STARS OF THE NEGRO LEAGUES

Satchel Paige

Legendary Pitcher

Enslow Publishing
101 W. 23rd Street
Suite 240
New York, NY 10011
USA
enslow.com

Hallie Murray

Published in 2020 by Enslow Publishing, LLC.
101 W. 23rd Street, Suite 240, New York, NY 10011

Cataloging-in-Publication Data

Names: Murray, Hallie.
Title: Satchel Paige: legendary pitcher / Hallie Murray
Description: New York : Enslow Publishing, 2020. | Series: Stars of the negro leagues | Includes bibliographic references and index. | Audience: Grades 7–12.
Identifiers: ISBN 9781978510593 (library bound) | ISBN 9781978510814 (pbk.)
Subjects: LCSH: Paige, Satchel, 1906–1982—Juvenile literature. | Pitchers (Baseball)—United States—Biography—Juvenile literature. | Baseball players—United States—Biography—Juvenile literature. | African American baseball players—United States—Biography—Juvenile literature. | Negro leagues—History—Juvenile literature. | Discrimination in sports—United States—History—Juvenile literature.
Classification: LCC GV865.P3 M87 2020 | DDC 796.357092/2 [B]—dc23

Printed in the United States of America

To Our Readers: We have done our best to make sure all website addresses in this book were active and appropriate when we went to press. However, the author and the publisher have no control over and assume no liability for the material available on those websites or on any websites they may link to. Any comments or suggestions can be sent by email to customerservice@enslow.com.

Portions of this book originally appeared in *Satchel Paige* by Julie Schmidt.

Photo Credits: Cover, p. 3 (inset photo Satchel Paige), pp. 33, 40–41, 49, 56–57, 63, 72, 77 Transcendental Graphics/Getty Images; cover, pp. 3, 7, 11, 25, 43, 60, 74 (background), pp. 12–13, 18–19 Library of Congress Prints and Photographs Division; cover, p. 3 (bat and ball) Mike Flippo/Shutterstock.com; pp. 9, 30–31, 38–39 National Baseball Hall of Fame and Museum; pp. 16–17 Corbis Historical/Getty Images; pp. 22–23 IanDagnall Computing/Alamy Stock Photo; p. 27 The Picture Art Collection/Alamy Stock Photo; pp. 36–37 Teenie Harris Archive/Carnegie Museum of Art/Carnegie Museum of Art/Getty Images; pp. 44–45 Vince Compagnone/Los Angeles Times/Getty Images; pp. 46–47 Hulton Deutsch/Corbis Historical/Getty Images; pp. 52–53 Bettmann/Getty Images; pp. 61, 83 © AP Images; p. 65 George Strock/The LIFE Picture Collection/Getty Images; p. 69 New York Daily News Archive/Getty Images; p. 80 Pictorial Parade/Archive Photos/Getty Images; p. 85 Lou Requena/Major League Baseball/Getty Images; cover, pp. 1, 3 (baseball graphic) Kano07/Shutterstock.com; interior pages (glove) Sergiy1975/Shutterstock.com; interior pages (diamond graphic) Viktorija Reuta/Shutterstock.com.

STARS OF THE NEGRO LEAGUES

Satchel Paige

Legendary Pitcher

Contents

Introduction

On July 7, 1948, Satchel Paige was forty-two years old, at least according to most sources. He stood on a pitcher's mound in the middle of a baseball diamond, just like the countless pitcher's mounds in countless diamonds he'd stood on over the course of his long pitching career in the Negro Leagues. But today, something was different. Today was the day he'd been waiting for his entire life: the chance to try out for a major league team.

Just one year earlier, Jackie Robinson had broken the Major League Baseball color line and become the first black player on a major league team as a first baseman for the Brooklyn Dodgers. He was twenty-eight years old. Since that moment, people had been waiting with bated breath for Satchel Paige to join a major league team. Paige was thirteen years older than Robinson and a better player by almost every measure. Many people had assumed Paige would be the first black player in the majors, including

Paige himself, but he lacked the right temperament. He was cocky and sometimes a poor teammate. He didn't seem to think he needed to practice or exercise to stay in shape like other players. The thing that frustrated his managers and teammates most was that he was right: despite his arrogance and rash behavior off-field, Satchel Paige was the best pitcher in the Negro Leagues, and according to many sources, the best pitcher in baseball history.

In July 1948, Paige finally had the opportunity to demonstrate his talents in a tryout for the major leagues. The manager of the Cleveland Indians, Bill Veeck, had been a fan of Paige's for a long time, but the Indians' manager, Lou Boudreau, had doubts. Boudreau knew Paige was a great pitcher, but he thought Paige was too old to still be competitive against major league hitters. Paige also didn't have the best reputation. As a compromise, Paige would try out for Boudreau personally by pitching to him for ten minutes and attempting to strike him out.

When Paige got out onto the field, Veeck and Boudreau were waiting. Boudreau asked Paige if he could still pitch. Paige admitted that he couldn't throw as fast as he used to, but he could still throw as fast as any other pitcher, and he had better control than anyone else. Boudreau went to the plate, and Paige started to pitch. Every ball Paige threw sailed directly over the base into Boudreau's mitt. Then Paige decided he needed an extra challenge.

In his typical cocky fashion, he stopped pitching, walked over to the plate, and laid a small handkerchief upon it. He then proceeded to put nine out of ten pitches over the handkerchief. His throws were accurate beyond belief. Some people say he learned his accuracy by using a bottle cap

Satchel Paige pitching circa 1941 in a New York Black Yankees uniform. Paige was one of the best-known Negro League players and the first Negro League player to be inducted into the Baseball Hall of Fame.

placed on the ground as a target. Then Boudreau picked up a bat to see if he could hit any of these incredibly accurate pitches. Out of twenty pitches, he only got one good hit.

Even Boudreau's biggest doubts couldn't blind him to the fact that Paige was still amazingly skilled, and Paige signed to that Indians that day. He was the oldest rookie in major league history. Paige considered making it to the majors the greatest achievement of his life. But he'd had an amazing career before that fateful July day and would go on to other phenomenal achievements after. He was the first pre-1974 Negro League player to be inducted into the National Baseball Hall of Fame, for good reason. Paige's impressive career spanned nearly forty years of pitching, but it began, in many ways, with his childhood in Mobile, Alabama.

Chapter 1

The Early Years

Although Leroy "Satchel" Paige is one of the most famous players to come out of the Negro Leagues, no one is quite sure when he was born. Most official records go by a birth certificate filed in Mobile, Alabama, for a boy named Leroy Paige. This would put his date of birth at July 7, 1906. But Paige and his mother could never be sure that was really his birth certificate, and other claims put his date of birth as early as 1900.

The fact that no one knew exactly how old Paige was made him seem mysterious to both his fans and peers, as though he were ageless, or somehow immortal. This impression was reinforced by his long career as a pitcher. It sometimes seemed like he would never stop playing baseball and would keep striking out players far younger than he was, long past the age most people retired. Which is basically of what he did. For forty years, Paige's legendary pitching struck out batters from the Negro Leagues to the majors.

A Childhood in Alabama

Although the date of his birth is uncertain, it is known that Leroy Paige's father, John, was a gardener, and his mother, Lula, was a laundress. John frequently left home, and he did not contribute much to the family in the way of money. He died when Leroy was eighteen. It was Lula who was the main breadwinner. And it was Lula who was mostly responsible for raising the couple's twelve children. Lula was a strong-willed, church-going woman, and she tried hard to keep her children in line.

The Paiges lived in a four-room "shotgun" house (a long, narrow house in which all the rooms are lined up off to one side of a hallway) in a poor black neighborhood on the south side of Mobile. Life was hard for many black people in Mobile at this time. The city was segregated, and black residents had to deal with racist Jim Crow laws (which enforced segregation and other forms of racial discrimination) and limited opportunities to find good jobs.

Like other families in their neighborhood, the Paiges did not have much money, and Leroy had to work to help his mother buy food for the family. One of his jobs was to carry suitcases ("satchels") for passengers at the Mobile railway station. Leroy was paid ten cents a bag, and he wanted to make as much money as he could, so he rigged together a contraption consisting of a pole and some rope which

A shotgun house is a narrow home with rooms arranged one after the other. This style of house is usually said to have originated in New Orleans.

allowed him to carry three or four bags at a time. He carried so many bags at once that the other porters said he looked like a "walking satchel tree." People say that is how Leroy got the nickname Satchel.

Leroy was a student at the Council School, a school for black children, but he frequently skipped his classes.

However, he did play baseball for his school team. Leroy had a powerful arm. He could throw rocks so hard that he once killed a chicken from thirty feet away. This strength and accuracy would prove to be very useful in his pitching career.

Unfortunately, while his baseball playing was improving, Leroy got into a lot of trouble off the field. Despite Lula's efforts to discipline him, he took part in many rock-throwing fights with neighborhood gangs. Usually, Leroy's black gang fought against a white gang from another neighborhood. Leroy became known as one of the most dangerous members of his gang because he could hit anyone at whom he aimed a rock.

When Leroy was twelve years old, he was caught stealing toy rings from a store. The storeowner took him to the police station, and Leroy was arrested. The court decided to send him to reform school. Leroy was sentenced to spend the rest of his childhood at the Industrial School for Negro Children at Mount Meigs, Alabama.

Life at Reform School

Leroy was frightened. It was the first time he had ever been away from home. He would not be allowed to visit his family in Mobile until his eighteenth birthday, which was still five years away. Also, he thought he might be treated badly at Mount Meigs by faculty and students alike. Strict discipline was enforced at the school, and students had to work in the fields for their keep.

Yet in later years, Leroy said that he considered himself lucky to have been sent to the school. Unlike at home, he was fed regular meals, and he got a lot of attention from the staff. In addition to his schoolwork, Leroy sang in the school

Finding the Right Word

At this time in the United States, "Negro" was the generally accepted term for African Americans. It comes from the Spanish word for "black." Both black and white people used it, and it did not yet carry racist connotations. During the civil rights movement of the 1950s and 1960s, however, many people began to push back against the use of "negro" because they felt that it was too much of a reminder of the horrible conditions black people faced during slavery and the Jim Crow era. In 2016, President Barack Obama signed legislation removing the words "Negro" and "Oriental" from federal laws.

Today, the word "negro" is used almost exclusively in a historical sense, like when discussing the Negro Leagues. Instead, the best term for a person today would be "African American" or "black," depending on the context or the individual's preference.

Pickup baseball was popular among kids of all races and socioeconomic classes. In this photo, junior high students in Washington, DC, watch as one of their peers hits the ball.

choir, played the drums in the school band, and did woodworking. Most importantly, he played baseball.

The baseball coach at the Industrial School, Edward Byrd, soon discovered that he had a natural pitcher on his team. Leroy could not throw a curveball, but his fastball was hard and accurate. Byrd helped Leroy make his fastball even better.

Of his years in reform school, Leroy would later say, "It got me away from the bums. It gave me a chance to polish up my baseball game. It gave me some schooling I'd of never taken if I wasn't made to go to class."

As he would do repeatedly throughout his life, at boarding school, Satchel Paige turned adversity to his advantage. In addition to receiving an education and much-needed adult attention at the Industrial School for Negro Children, it was there that he discovered the gift that would see him through the

A street in an African American neighborhood of the port city of Mobile, Alabama, where Satchel Paige was born. In the early twentieth century, the city's main industries were shipbuilding and steel production.

many long years ahead and establish him as a legend: his extraordinary skill as a pitcher.

Joining the Mobile Tigers

At the end of 1923, Paige was released from the Industrial School, and went back to Mobile. Paige's mother soon informed him that he needed to find work to help out with the family finances. There weren't many jobs available in the city, especially for a young black man with a reform school record. Paige knew, however, that there was one job he could easily get: playing baseball. Paige was certain he had more than enough talent to play professionally.

Leroy's brother, Wilson, nicknamed Paddlefoot, was a pitcher and catcher for a local semiprofessional team, the Mobile Tigers. Leroy challenged the Tigers' coach to face him in batting practice. The coach could not hit a single one of Paige's pitches, and he was hired on the spot.

Paige soon became the Tigers' star player. He perfected the pitching techniques he had learned at the Industrial School, and no one could hit his fastball. At the same time, he began to develop the showmanship for which he would be famous throughout his career. By walking slowly and casually to the mound, he created a sense of suspense before he even threw a single pitch. This was the calm before the storm of his fastball. He also had a way with words and got plenty of laughs from the crowd when he bragged about his pitching and talked trash to the other players.

Paige became known as a pitcher who could pull off daring and imaginative stunts. Halfway through the 1926 season, while he played for another semipro team, the Chattanooga Black Lookouts, Paige's teammates committed several errors. The bases were loaded, and the fans booed Paige's team. Sensing that his team was losing fan support, Paige decided to take drastic measures to win back the crowd. He ordered his outfielders to sit down behind the pitching mound. Then, with no one on the diamond in a position to field the ball, Paige struck out the next batter. The crowd, back on his side, cheered wildly, and rumors quickly began to spread about this crazy young pitcher.

In spite of his success, Paige was frustrated because he was not making enough money. Although the Tigers did not like it, Paige would pitch for other teams if they offered him enough money. In addition to pitching, Paige took a job sweeping the stadium of the Mobile Bears, a white minor league team.

The white players had heard about Paige's pitching for the Tigers, and they asked him to give them a demonstration. They were stunned by his skill. After the demonstration, one of the players told him it was too bad he was not white. If he had been white, he would have been able to play in the major leagues. This was the first time Paige had heard these words, but it would not be the last.

A Segregated Nation

Baseball had not always been segregated. The game was invented in the 1840s, and it became popular during the Civil War. Right after the war, black slaves were set free. Black men were allowed to vote for the first time, and African Americans were elected to positions in local governments. It was during this time that some talented black baseball players also began to play on the same teams as whites.

Jim Crow laws made it legal to have separate facilities for black and white Americans, including bus station waiting rooms, like this one in Durham, North Carolina, in 1940.

It didn't take long for things to change, however. Throughout the late nineteenth and early twentieth centuries, Jim Crow was established all over the country, particularly in the southern states. These laws created a system of segregation in the United States similar to apartheid in South Africa, where black people were separated from white people. Under Jim Crow, there were separate schools, hotels, restaurants, water fountains, and restrooms for white and black people. These facilities were supposed to be "separate but equal," but in actuality the facilities for African Americans were lower in quality than the ones for white people.

Jim Crow had an effect on baseball, too. Many white players did not want to continue to play with or against black players. In the 1887–1888 season, the International League, one of the organizations that controlled baseball, changed its rules, formally shutting black players out of white baseball teams. Suddenly there were no teams on which African Americans could play. They had no choice but to set up their own baseball teams and to play against each other.

Chapter 2

Paige's Professional Career Begins

In the early twentieth century, white baseball was structured pretty much the same way professional baseball is today. Professional white teams were formally organized into two major leagues, the National League and the American League. Minor league teams would funnel their best young talent up to the major leagues when the players seemed ready to succeed at the next level. There were also semipro teams, in which players had other jobs and only played baseball part-time. Baseball players usually started their careers in the semipro and minor leagues. In many cases, older major league players would end their careers on minor league teams once their skills began to drop off. In this way, their professional baseball careers would come full circle.

Black baseball, on the other hand, was less structured, particularly in its early years. While white baseball teams stuck with the loose organization and rules that had developed in baseball over its first thirty or so years of existence in the United States, black players had to create new teams and organizations from scratch. As such, there were few regulations and little oversight. The terms of a contract were rarely followed. Players often "jumped" or switched teams the minute they were offered more money than they were currently being paid. There were also fewer rules and regulations in black baseball.

Given the large number of talented black baseball players who were shut out of the white major leagues, and given the enormous African American fan base, it was only a matter of time before black teams followed the model of the National and American Leagues and became more professional. In this new environment, Satchel Paige flourished. He began to make a name for himself even in white sports circles. The Negro Leagues would also provide him eventual passage into baseball's promised land—an integrated major league and the National Baseball Hall of Fame.

The First of the Negro Leagues

Starting in the late 1880s, several attempts were made to organize the black teams into leagues. None were really successful. This would change in 1920, however, when Andrew "Rube" Foster established the first Negro League.

Foster, a former star pitcher and famous baseball personality, was the manager of the Chicago American Giants. He had a lot of power in the world of black baseball. Foster felt that if black baseball was more organized, African American teams eventually might be able to play professional championships against white major league

In the first decade of the 1900s, Rube Foster was known as a pitcher, but today he is best remembered as the founder of the Negro National League, the first lasting league of the Negro Leagues.

teams, thus gaining access to the money and prestige available in the major league world.

Foster asked seven other Midwestern teams to join him in establishing the Negro National League. The Negro National League had strict rules, just like the white major leagues, and it fined players, owners, and managers who did not follow these rules. Foster was to play a leading role in this league, and his team, the American Giants, won the League's first three championships.

At first, fans flocked to the Negro National League games. Inspired by the league's profits, other black baseball leagues formed, including the Negro Southern League and the Eastern Colored League. However, all of these leagues ran into problems fairly quickly. Some teams were much better than others, meaning that certain teams always won the championships. Generally, the wealthy teams were the ones that dominated the leagues because they could afford the best players and equipment. As in earlier days, players broke the rules of the Negro National League—and their contracts—to switch to the teams that could pay them better. Because there was an imbalance of wealth among teams, the richer teams could lure away talented players. At first, owners tried to maintain some order on their teams, but they were unable to keep it up. Player morale was low due to this inequity and lack of stability.

The strain of keeping his league together began to affect Rube Foster. In 1927, he suffered a mental breakdown and had to be hospitalized. He died a few years later. Once Foster was no longer part of the scene, the Negro league he had established fell apart completely.

Paige in the Negro Leagues

Satchel Paige's career in the Negro Leagues would blossom in this atmosphere of relative chaos. Late in 1926, when Paige was still playing for the Mobile Tigers, a scout for the Chattanooga Black Lookouts came to watch him play. The Black Lookouts were a professional team in the Negro Southern League, and they offered Paige a pitching position. He accepted the job and won almost every game he started for the Chattanooga Black Lookouts.

In 1927, the Chattanooga Black Lookouts traded Paige to the Birmingham Black Barons, the best team in the Negro Southern League. Paige spent the next three years with the Barons. He developed several unique pitches, including the "two-hump blooper" (a changeup), the "Little Tom" (a medium fastball), and the "Long Tom" (a hard fastball).

Things really started happening for Paige in 1929, when the Nashville Elite Giants acquired him. Despite their name, the Giants actually played in Cleveland, Ohio. Playing for them brought Paige to the attention of major league owners and baseball writers who seldom ventured into the South.

The Giants were only one of the many teams that wanted Paige's services. After the regular season ended, Paige continued to play baseball. Because of his growing fame as a pitcher, Paige was tapped to pitch for the Baltimore Black Sox in a series of exhibition games against a white major league team, the Babe Ruth All-Stars. Even though black and white players could not play together during the regular professional season, they were free to play exhibition games against each other when the regular season was over. These interracial games were very popular with fans.

CHICAGO
CHICAGO
CHICAGO
CHICAGO

The Chicago American Giants were owned and managed by Rube Foster from 1911 to 1926. The team was a major force in Foster's Negro National League. Foster is in the center of the back row.

Barnstorming

Since many black teams did not own their own stadiums, they could schedule games in white teams' stadiums only when they were not being used. It was impossible to schedule enough regular games to keep the teams going, so most of them had to barnstorm. Barnstorming teams traveled from town to town, playing exhibition games against local teams in order to attract enough fans and play enough games to make ends meet. Black teams usually traveled in buses, sometimes playing two or three games in different locations within one day. Sometimes, when the town had no hotels or restaurants that would serve black customers, the players had to eat cold sandwiches and sleep on the playing fields. Despite all of its challenges, barnstorming could be a great way to travel the country and gain fans in all different places.

Babe Ruth aims at an incoming pitch in 1927 at Yankee Stadium. Ruth is one of the most famous baseball players ever, best known as a slugger and outfielder on the New York Yankees from 1920 to 1934.

To his great disappointment, Paige never got to pitch against the Babe, but he did very well against the rest of Ruth's team, going so far as to strike out twenty-two players in one game. Exhilarated by his success against white players, Paige was eager to take on new challenges.

Gus Greenlee and the Pittsburgh Crawfords

The late 1920s and early 1930s were a tough period for black teams, which again fell into disorganization following the failure of Foster's Negro National League. In addition, the Great Depression meant that many fans were too poor to buy baseball tickets. However, as soon as the American economy began to recover from the Depression, people began to talk about starting up a new Negro National League.

The first man to succeed at this endeavor was a rich black businessman named Gus Greenlee. Greenlee owned the Pittsburgh Crawfords, one of the best black teams in the country. Hoping that local black fans would buy lots of tickets for his games, Greenlee started the second Negro National League in 1933. This league survived—in one form or another—until 1948.

Greenlee recruited the best players he could find. One of these players was an up-and-coming pitcher from the South...Satchel Paige. Paige was happy to join the Crawfords in 1931. This was the big break he had been hoping for. His new teammates included big Negro League stars like Josh Gibson, Cool Papa Bell, and Judy Johnson. Playing in such company, he knew that real stardom was within his reach. It was while playing for the Crawfords that Paige enjoyed his first real taste of fame and popularity; in other words,

A New Kind of Pitcher

Despite all the great players on Gus Greenlee's team, it soon became obvious that Satchel Paige was something special. His "pea ball," or "bee ball" as he liked to call it (because of the way it hummed), was a very powerful fastball that was difficult for batters to see as it went across the plate. Paige put a peculiar wobble on his pitches. Because of the ball's strange motion, hitters couldn't tell what sort of pitch was coming their way. By the time they figured it out, the ball was already in the catcher's hand. Paige's signature windups, like the Model T and the windmill, were fun to watch, as were his stunts on the field. The fans loved him.

the attention of the national press and the American public.

Professional Success; Personal Struggles

One night, after Paige led his team to a big victory over the Homestead Grays, Greenlee held a big party in his honor at his restaurant, the Crawford Grill. Paige spied a shy, pretty waitress standing on the other side of the room. Her name was Janet Howard.

Soon, Paige and Janet began to date. Janet didn't like all the traveling that Paige had to do. However, it was necessary for Paige to keep moving around—as he had earlier in his career—in order to keep pitching for all the teams who wanted him and to make enough money to cover his expenses.

Even though he was being paid more money than any of the other players, Paige did not save much of it. He was always running out of cash and asking for advances from Greenlee. Greenlee warned him that he should start saving, but dating Janet only made matters worse. The only money Paige did not spend immediately was the monthly allowance he sent to his mother in Mobile.

Gus Greenlee poses with a woman in his Pittsburgh establishment, Crawford Grill, in 1943. Greenlee was a racketeer (gangster) who used his money to support the Pittsburgh Crawfords baseball team.

Baseball games were major social events, and tons of baseball fans, especially African American fans, attended Negro League games. This full stadium is likely in Kansas City.

In general, Paige was not known for his discipline and seriousness. He was unreliable, and he angered team owners and fans by showing up late or by not showing up at all. Everyone tolerated Paige's behavior, though, because he was such a good pitcher and the Crawfords could not win without him.

In 1934, Paige had one of the best seasons of his career, allowing only 85 hits in 154 innings. As one of the best—and the most popular—pitchers in the Negro Leagues, Paige was a shoe-in for a pitching spot on the East team for the second annual East-West All-Star Game. Paige later said that as he was walking out to the mound to start pitching, he heard a fan say, "It's Paige. Good-bye ballgame."

Paige didn't disappoint the fan. He saved the day for his team, allowing only two hits in four innings. This exciting game was one of the first Negro League games to be covered by both the black and the white sports press. Some white fans heard about Satchel Paige for the first time.

After Paige's All-Star victory, Greenlee was even more eager to hold on to him. He quickly re-signed Paige to a new two-year contract.

Paige spent many seasons playing winter ball in Latin America, including a stint in the Mexican league in 1938. Twenty years later, he would return to Mexico to act in the film *The Wonderful Country*. Here he is on set.

Meanwhile, Paige and Janet's relationship took a new turn, and later that year (1934), the couple got married. However, Paige began to have serious money problems again. Married life, it turned out, was even more expensive than dating. As usual, he went to Gus Greenlee to ask for an advance. Thinking that he now had Paige locked into a contract, Greenlee refused this latest request for money.

Paige was outraged. He decided to take the first decent job offer he got, and he didn't have to wait long. A few days later, he broke his contract with Greenlee and signed on with the Bismarck Baseball Club, a semipro team in North Dakota. Furious, Greenlee tried to arrange for Paige to be banned from playing on any Negro League team in the future. Paige didn't care. He and Janet packed their bags and left for North Dakota.

Chapter 3

Searching for an Integrated Team

Unlike professional baseball and American society in general, semipro ball was integrated, and Paige found himself playing with both white and black players on the North Dakotan team. Unfortunately, the Bismarck Baseball Club was not very good, but the experience of playing on an integrated team would help ease Paige's eventual entry into the major leagues. In 1935, Paige led the Bismarck team alongside the famous Negro League player Ted "Double Duty" Radcliffe, who had played on the Crawfords with him. Radcliffe's nickname, "Double Duty," came from the 1932 Negro League World Series, when he played catcher with Paige pitching for the first game, then pitched the game immediately following for two back-to-back shutouts.

Paige was such a good pitcher that he'd become well-known among white baseball players as well as black players. There were many amazing players in the Negro Leagues, but few tried as hard as Paige to match up against white major leaguers. Paige wanted to try his skills against the best hitters of the day—white or black—and by jumping from team to team, he actually did manage to pitch against some of the top hitters in the Negro Leagues and the MLB. But it wouldn't ever feel fair until Paige and other black players were finally let into the major leagues, a moment that was still a long way off.

Baseball in Bismarck

The Bismarck Baseball Club was not very good, but it was integrated. This was the first time in Paige's life that he would play on the same team as white players. The team's managers hoped that a talented black pitcher would boost ticket sales to their games, and they were right. Paige won all eighteen of the games he played for the team, and as usual, the fans were crazy about him.

Janet was not too thrilled about the move to North Dakota, especially after she discovered that none of the white residents of Bismarck wanted to rent out their houses to a black couple. The newlyweds eventually had to move into an abandoned railway car, the only residence that was available to them.

At first, Paige's white teammates did not like their cocky new pitcher very much.

The Bismarck Baseball Club in 1935. Satchel Paige is in the center of the back row, with Ted "Double Duty" Radcliffe on the far right in the back row.

During one game, after Paige yelled at them for missing a few routine fly balls, his outfielders rebelled. They refused to go out to field when a new inning started. The fans cheered, thinking the whole thing was a stunt like the one

Paige had pulled back in Mobile when he had ordered his outfield to sit down behind the pitching mound. Paige had to apologize before the outfielders would take their positions again.

The only people in Bismarck with whom Paige really felt comfortable were the Sioux Indians. He visited them often on their reservation outside the city. Paige liked to tell the story of the day he visited an elderly Sioux man who raised rattlesnakes. The man gave Paige a special ointment to use as an antidote whenever he was bitten by the snakes. For the rest of his life, Paige claimed to use the ointment as a salve for his pitching arm, and he credited it with contributing to his longevity as a pitcher.

The Satchel Paige All-Stars

When the season in Bismarck ended, Paige and Janet left North Dakota. Janet went back to Pittsburgh alone, while Paige formed a team of his own, the Satchel Paige All-Stars. Paige had enjoyed barnstorming against the Babe Ruth

President Franklin D. Roosevelt shakes hands with Chief Noal Bad Wound of the Sioux Nation in Bismarck, North Dakota, in 1936. Paige spent most of his time with the American Indians who lived in Bismarck.

All-Stars back in 1929, and he wanted to repeat the experience with other white major league teams. There was no shortage of potential opponents.

Major leaguers welcomed the opportunity to make some extra money on off-season exhibition games, and they were especially eager to try their luck at hitting Paige's famous fastball, an opportunity they were denied during the baseball season because of segregation.

There were some differences in style between white major leaguers and the black players they played against in these exhibition games. By the 1930s, the major leagues had outlawed tampering with the ball and other practices of the old style of baseball play that was still legal in the Negro Leagues.

Another difference was that black players were often forced to be as skilled at entertainment as they were at baseball. During this time, because popular movies and radio shows cast African Americans in stereotypically clownish roles, managers of black teams hoped that more white fans would come to the games if their players performed amusing stunts. Also, when barnstorming black teams played white teams, jokes helped to smooth ruffled feathers and soothe any offended white people when the black teams won.

The challenge for black players was to ensure that even when they were forced to clown around, they kept playing good baseball. Satchel Paige was a master at maintaining this balance. It was because of this that he was so popular on the barnstorming circuit. People wanted excitement and entertainment at barnstorming games, and nobody could deliver both better than Paige.

Even if Paige and his All-Stars joked around on the field, they insisted on being treated with respect. While he was barnstorming, Paige always refused to play in towns that would not let black players sleep in their hotels.

Playing Against MLB Legends

One of the Satchel Paige All-Stars' barnstorming rivals was a team led by the major league pitcher Jay "Dizzy"

Paige *(left)* chats with Jay "Dizzy" Dean of the St. Louis Cardinals at an exhibition game in 1936 at Wrigley Field in Chicago.

Dean. Dizzy and Paige had a lot in common. Dizzy liked to throw fastballs, and he was an uneducated, though slick and entertaining, showman from the South, just like Paige.

The two pitchers had a friendly but competitive relationship. Of the six games they played against each other in one tournament, Paige won four, and Dizzy had to admit that Paige was a better pitcher than he was. Years later, Dizzy wrote in an article that Satchel Paige, with his long arms and odd windup and delivery, was the best pitcher he had ever seen. "If Satch and I was pitching the same team," he once claimed, "we'd clinch the pennant by the Fourth of July and go fishing until World Series time."

Dizzy Dean wasn't the only famous white player Paige pitched against during this period of his career. In one memorable exhibition game, Paige struggled to prevent Dick Bartell's All-Stars from defeating his own team, which consisted of himself, another Negro Leaguer, and an assortment of inexperienced semipro players. Paige struck out as many of his opponents as he could and did his best to hit the ball whenever he was at bat. He even coached his inexperienced teammates from first base when he wasn't actually playing.

Despite his best efforts, however, an umpire called Paige out late in the game. Paige was rattled by this rare failure. In the next inning, Joe DiMaggio, who was about to move to New York to begin his legendary career with the Yankees, hit one of Paige's pitches, resulting in the winning home run. After the game, Paige heard DiMaggio say that he knew he could make it with the Yankees now, after finally getting a hit off "Ol' Satch." DiMaggio also went on the record as

Joltin' Joe DiMaggio

Many consider Joe DiMaggio one of the greatest baseball players of all time. He was a center fielder who spent his entire professional career, from 1936 to 1951, playing for the New York Yankees. One of his most famous achievements was setting the record for the longest hitting streak in Major League Baseball: fifty-six games, meaning DiMaggio got at least one base hit each game for fifty-six games straight. This record still stands today. He also set a record on the Yankees for most home runs in a rookie season (twenty-nine), which stood for over seventy years until Aaron Judge broke it in his 2017 rookie season. Among non-baseball fans, DiMaggio is best remembered for his brief marriage to actress Marilyn Monroe. It lasted for less than a year, but DiMaggio never remarried, and he was Monroe's main support in the last years of her life. DiMaggio passed away in 1999 from lung cancer.

Joe DiMaggio of the New York Yankees is pictured here hitting a home run during a game against the Philadelphia Athletics in 1939.

saying that Paige was "the best and fastest pitcher I've ever faced."

In fact, Paige is said to be the reason that baseball players wear plastic helmets today. For a 1936 barnstorming game, a white team from Borger, Texas, wore helmets around their caps so that they wouldn't get hurt if one of Satchel's fastballs hit them in the head. It was the first time any baseball player had worn protection on his head.

Major League Dreams

Paige's spectacular performance against white major leaguers impressed sports journalists. Some of them even wrote about what a shame it was that great players like him were barred from the major leagues because of racism in American baseball.

Paige pretended he was perfectly happy where he was, but in actuality, he was hoping to be asked to try out for the majors. He was flattered by the compliments he was getting from famous white players like Dizzy Dean, and he couldn't help resenting the fact that he wasn't allowed to play with them all the time. He wanted the money and prestige that were available in the major leagues *and* the social acceptance of black people that integrated play would represent.

Satchel Paige also wanted to prove that he could strike out white major leaguers under any circumstances. It was easier to strike out major leaguers in off-season exhibition games—when they were tired and out of shape—than it was to strike them out during the season, when they were at the top of their game and were chasing the championship. Until he pitched in the majors, Paige wouldn't be able to prove to the world that he really was the best pitcher around.

Between the Crawfords and Latin America

The attention Paige was getting from the world of white baseball made Greenlee change his mind about banning Paige from the Negro Leagues, and he soon asked Paige to come back to the Crawfords. At the same time, Greenlee put pressure on other Negro League teams to refuse to hire him, limiting Paige's ability to sign up with other teams. Paige felt that he had no choice but to agree to pitch for the Crawfords during the 1936 season.

Despite Greenlee's renewed attempts to lock him in, Paige didn't stay with the Crawfords for long. In 1937, at spring training in New Orleans, he was approached by two agents of the president of the Dominican Republic, Rafael Trujillo. Baseball was and continues to be extremely popular in the Caribbean and in Latin America, and local politicians used baseball teams to build popularity with their constituents. Trujillo was facing a strong challenge from another political party and was looking for an opportunity to polish his image. He wanted to make sure his baseball team, Los Dragones, was the best in the country, and he was willing to spend a lot of money to do it. One of the players he most wanted to recruit was Satchel Paige.

Paige had a pretty good deal with the Crawfords, but the two Dominican men made him an offer he couldn't refuse. For what amounted to $9,000 for a few weeks of work—more money than he'd ever been paid before— he agreed to sign on with Trujillo's team.

After his brief stint with Los Dragones, Paige returned to the United States and discovered that once again, Greenlee had forgiven him for breaking his contract, and he went back to pitching for the Crawfords. Over the summer, Paige barnstormed against another famous white pitcher, Bob Feller, and traveled around for a while with a team from the House of David, a fundamentalist religious group.

In 1938, Paige broke his Crawfords contract again and went to play for a baseball team in Mexico. Greenlee's patience was finally exhausted; he traded Paige to the Newark Eagles. Paige decided to stay in Mexico, however, and he never played for the Eagles. Unfortunately, Mexico was to prove bad for Paige's health.

Throughout his career, Paige had been careful to treat his pitching arm well. He never pitched without loosening up first. He always wore thick, long-sleeved shirts on the mound, and he took hot baths before games so that he would never be cold and stiff. He also claimed to frequently use his Sioux snake ointment, which seemed to soothe and loosen his weary, aging muscles. Paige thought his arm would last forever, even though he used it practically every day. That summer in Mexico, however, he was proven wrong.

House of David Bas

The House of David was a religious society founded by Benjamin and Mary Purnell in Michigan. Members grew their hair and beards long to honor the God of Israel. Benjamin Purnell believed strongly in the importance of athletics and encouraged House of David members to play sports, especially baseball.

The Fall of a Pitcher

The House of David was a religious order that demanded that all its male converts grow beards. The order's baseball team helped to spread the word about its beliefs. Paige could only grow a mustache, so his teammates lent him a long, red false beard. He got very upset one day when his arm got tangled up in the beard, causing an important pitch to go awry.

One day, he began to feel an ache in his arm, but he kept pitching because he was being paid by the game and didn't want to lose any money. The pain didn't go away, and his manager finally told him to take the afternoon off. Paige had a few drinks of tequila and went to bed. When he got up the next morning, he couldn't lift his arm. He rushed to the ballpark and tried to throw a few pitches. To his horror, he realized he could not throw a ball farther than a few feet.

The team's manager called in some doctors, but no one could figure out what was wrong with Paige's arm. After a few days, he was sent home. But American doctors couldn't help him either. One even told him that he would never pitch again.

Paige couldn't believe what had happened. Just a few weeks earlier, everyone had wanted to hire him. But now, with his pitching arm gone, no one was interested in him. He was still only about thirty-two years old, and he could have managed a baseball team or become a coach. However, Paige's years of breaking contracts and failing to show up for games came back to haunt him. His old contacts in the Negro Leagues did not feel like doing him any favors.

Depressed and lonely, Paige couldn't bring himself to go back to Janet. He felt like a failure. And not only that, he was experiencing money problems again, this time with no hope of finding a quick solution in terms of getting a new job. The man who used to have his pick of job offers in the United States and beyond suddenly found that his phone had stopped ringing. With no savings or prospects, he had to pawn his belongings, including his fancy car and fishing equipment, just to survive.

Chapter 4

A Fresh Start

It seemed like the end of the road for Satchel Paige. He could no longer rely on his pitching arm, which had been his sole source of income and the cause of his fame. But just when he was losing hope, Paige got a call from J.L. Wilkinson, the owner of the Kansas City Monarchs. The Monarchs were the best black team in the Midwest, and Wilkinson was the kind of owner who looked out for players who were going through a streak of bad luck or were nearing the end of their careers. It wasn't clear which Paige was, but regardless, he clearly needed Wilkinson's kind assistance.

Since Paige could not really pitch, Wilkinson gave him a spot on one of the Monarchs' traveling teams. He began to barnstorm with them. It was an embarrassing time for Paige. Fans came to the games, expecting to see the old, spectacular Satchel Paige. They weren't impressed with what he had turned into since his arm injury. He even overheard one boy ask his dad how he had ever gotten anyone out.

Paige poses in the dugout at Yankee Stadium in 1942 during a game between the Kansas City Monarchs and the New York Cuban Stars.

But the arm injury would soon disappear just as mysteriously as it had happened, and his baseball career eventually rose to new heights. For a few months with the traveling team, Paige took it easy, pitching a couple of innings here and there. Then one day, he was throwing a few warm-up pitches. All of a sudden, his arm stopped hurting. He called his catcher and told him to get ready to catch a fastball—the first he'd thrown since his injury. It sailed into the catcher's glove with speed and power.

Paige's arm was back. Jubilant, he called Wilkinson with the news that very evening. The owner told him that he could join the Monarchs for the 1939 season. Far from having reached the end of the road, Paige found himself poised for a new level of success and recognition, and it looked like Wilkinson had made a good investment by betting on the once down-and-out pitcher.

Into the Spotlight

Soon Paige was at the top of his game. Because the Kansas City Monarchs were one of the first teams to play night baseball, using portable spotlights that they took with them from town to town, Paige sometimes had to play three games in one day. Even though he was pitching more than ever, it was as if nothing had ever happened to his arm. He led the Monarchs to four straight Negro American League championship victories in the early forties.

In one legendary game in 1942, the Monarchs faced the Homestead Grays. Paige loved to tell the story of what happened when he faced his old teammate, Josh Gibson, in this game. Paige had always wanted to prove that he was a better pitcher than Gibson was a hitter, and he made a $5 bet with Gibson that he would be able to strike him out.

By the seventh inning of the game, however, Paige had not yet succeeded in his mission. He decided to take drastic and risky measures to ensure that he won the bet. There were two outs and two batters up before Gibson's turn at bat, so Paige decided to deliberately walk the two batters. His teammates thought he was crazy, because if Gibson hit a home run, the Grays would win the game. Nevertheless, Paige insisted. Gibson came up to the plate.

Paige with his teammate and occasional rival Josh Gibson in 1941. Gibson was known as a powerful slugger and excellent catcher. He passed away tragically at the age of thirty-five in 1947.

Amazingly, before each pitch, Paige told Gibson what kind of ball he was going to throw. He then pitched the ball, and Gibson missed it—three times in a row. The fans went wild. Paige had psyched Gibson out to win both his bet and the ball game.

During this phase of his career, Paige developed his famous "hesitation" pitch. He knew that his fastball wasn't quite as powerful as it had been before his injury, and he was getting older. Because of this, he decided he needed something extra to ensure that batters would keep missing his pitches. What Paige came up with was to begin putting his foot down before throwing the ball, making it look like he had already thrown it. Players would swing for the ball while Paige was still holding it in his hand.

Paige's experiences after his injury made him more careful about breaking contracts, and he did not want to treat Wilkinson badly. He wound up playing for the Monarchs, on and off, for the next eight years. Wilkinson also lent him out occasionally, and Paige continued to play for other teams off-season.

Meeting Lahoma Brown

Following his divorce from Janet in 1943, Paige returned to Kansas City, where one day he decided to go shopping in a drugstore. An attractive woman rang up his purchase. She didn't know who Paige was, and because his pride was hurt, he found an excuse to complain to the manager about her.

Later, Paige felt guilty about his rude behavior. He went back to the store again and again, each time asking to be served by the "half-smart girl," Lahoma Brown. Eventually, when it seemed like she had forgiven him, Paige asked her

Paige with then-wife Janet Howard in 1941. Their marriage ended in 1943, and Paige married his second wife, Lahoma Brown in 1947. His marriage to Lahoma lasted the rest of his life.

out to dinner. It was the beginning of a relationship that would last for the rest of Paige's life. Later, in his autobiography, Paige described Lahoma as the only woman who had ever been able to make him slow down and settle down.

The Challenges of Fame

Time, Life magazine, and the *Saturday Evening Post* all published profiles of Paige around this time. Although the profiles praised Paige's masterful pitching, they also stereotyped him as a crazy clown, a buffoonish entertainer, and an exotic witchdoctor. Much was made of the mystery of his age, his diet, his snake oil, and his fancy clothes.

In later years, Paige complained about the way these journalists made him look and sound peculiar. But at the time, he didn't try hard to convince them otherwise. The articles that were written about him made him into a household name all over the United States. And Paige knew that the more famous he was, the more money would come his way.

He was right. All the publicity Paige was receiving attracted more fans to baseball, and the Negro League managers rewarded him accordingly. His salary was almost $40,000 a year, making him the highest-paid athlete in the world at the time. Wilkinson even bought Paige his own private plane to take him from game to game.

The plane didn't work out very well. During Paige's first flight, the small plane was caught in a storm, and he refused to fly in it again. The pilot told him that if he missed the game the next day, he wouldn't get the $500 that he had been promised. Always reluctant to lose money, Paige agreed to try a second flight. This time, the plane sprung an oil leak. Paige was terrified that it would drop out of the sky. After the plane landed, he swore he would never board it again, and this time he meant it. The Monarchs ended up selling the plane.

Outside of the plane fiasco, Satchel Paige's career was back on track, and he was enjoying all of the accompanying success and publicity. Elsewhere in the world, however, the storm clouds of war were gathering. As dark a time as this was for the United States, World War II indirectly led to a development that many baseball players and fans had long wished for but rarely had believed possible: integration of the game. Though Paige would not be the first black player admitted to the major leagues, he would eventually benefit from the courageous trailblazing of Jackie Robinson and the Brooklyn Dodgers' owner, Branch Rickey. More than twenty years after becoming a professional baseball player, Paige would finally gain his long-deserved place in the major leagues.

Crossing the Color Line

The United States entered World War II in 1942, and many baseball players left to enlist in the armed forces. More than ever, the majors needed players of Paige's quality. Rumors began to circulate that Branch Rickey, the owner of the Brooklyn Dodgers, was planning to integrate his team. In October 1945, the news broke that Rickey had assigned a black player to the Montreal Royals, a minor league farm team for the Brooklyn Dodgers. The black player was Jackie Robinson, one of Paige's former teammates from the Monarchs.

Jackie Robinson

Jackie Robinson was a gifted athlete who was known for keeping his cool in difficult circumstances. In high school, Robinson was awarded varsity letters in four sports: baseball, football, basketball, and track. Robinson's high school sports were integrated, giving him early experience with handling the potential difficulties of being a black player on an integrated team. After attending University of California, Los Angeles (UCLA) for college, Robinson joined an integrated semiprofessional football team in Hawaii. Then Pearl Harbor happened, and Robinson was drafted to the military, where he was soon accepted into Officer Candidate School. In 1944, during his military service, Robinson was arrested for refusing to move to the back of a bus. He'd done nothing wrong, but this experience was one of many that gave Robinson the confidence and skills to calmly but firmly stand up to racist authority figures, qualities that Branch Rickey valued highly when looking for his first black player.

Jackie Robinson was the first black player in the major leagues when he joined the Brooklyn Dodgers in 1947. Here, he enters the Dodgers clubhouse still wearing his minor leagues Montreal Royals uniform.

Rickey had chosen the first black player very carefully. Everyone would be watching this man and looking for flaws. Robinson would have to put up with insults and abuse from racists who wanted to see him fail. Rickey wanted someone who could withstand the pressure. He also needed someone who would follow the rules and not embarrass him off the field. Robinson fit the bill in a way that Paige did not. He was young and college educated, a good all-around athlete. Robinson wasn't the best African American player, but he was very good. He was dignified, reserved, and dependable. He was a family man, and he didn't drink or stay out all night.

Paige, with his reputation for clowning, unreliability, and greed, was not the kind of man Rickey was looking for. Still, Paige was upset at the news about Robinson. Paige knew he was getting older and was not as good a pitcher as he used to be, but somehow he had still expected to be the first black player to break the color barrier.

Robinson played well, and in 1947, he was called up to the Dodgers. The experiment of introducing a black player into the majors was declared a success. More major league teams began to sign African American players.

Entering the Majors

In 1948, it was finally Paige's turn. Paige had a good relationship with Bill Veeck, the owner of the Cleveland Indians, a major league team. Veeck had wanted to hire Paige ever since he had seen him pitch in the early 1930s, and he had considered signing him right after Robinson was signed to the Dodgers. But, since Paige was getting older, Veeck was afraid people would see the hire as a publicity stunt.

Veeck changed his mind about hiring Paige when the Indians found themselves in need of a great pitcher to help them win the American League pennant. Veeck's scouts told him that Paige was still the best pitcher in the Negro Leagues. Veeck organized a tryout for Paige at the Indians' ballpark, and Paige passed the test with flying colors.

Paige knew that he might have lost some of his power, but he still had the moves to outsmart most batters. But he was very nervous. He was the oldest rookie in major league history, and people had high expectations based on his fame outside of the majors. At his first major league game against the St. Louis Browns, 35,000 fans came out to see the famous rookie pitch, and the pressure on Paige was enormous. When he was called to the mound, photographers rushed out onto the field to get pictures of him. Paige's stomach was acting up, and at first he was very stiff. But soon he loosened up, and he didn't allow any runs before he was taken out of the game.

Paige's playing suffered a blow when umpires banned one of his most powerful weapons, the hesitation pitch, a pitch that allowed him to compensate for his previously injured arm and slowing fastball. Nevertheless, in the games that followed, he managed a couple of shutouts and won six games out of seven, helping the Indians win the American League pennant and get into their first World Series in twenty-eight years. His earned run average (ERA) that season was 2.48, and he struck out enough batters to be named Rookie of the Year, an honor usually associated with youth and inexperience. This "rookie" was in his forties and had played professional baseball for more than twenty years!

Paige didn't let the pressures of the major leagues change him too much. He continued to enjoy life. He refused to exercise, he drank too much, and he frequently stayed out late. He also showed up late or missed games, just as he had in the Negro Leagues. But Lou Boudreau, the Indians' manager, was not as tolerant as the Negro League managers

Paige was the oldest rookie in the major leagues when he was signed to the Cleveland Indians in 1948. He is pictured here warming up in his Cleveland uniform at a game in 1948.

had been. He fined Paige for his rule breaking and allowed him to pitch in fewer and fewer games.

The situation was so bad that it didn't look like Boudreau would let Paige play in the 1948 World Series. Paige sat through the first few games of the series, itching to pitch, but Boudreau ignored him. In the fifth game, however, Boudreau had no choice. He went through all the other pitchers on his bench before he finally called Paige to the mound, much to the delight of the crowd. Hassled by the umpires for his unorthodox pitching style, Paige only pitched for two-thirds of an inning before he was taken out of the game. But that was enough to make him officially the first black pitcher to play in a major league World Series.

The Indians won the World Series that year, but things didn't improve for Paige. He wasn't doing well physically, and soon, Boudreau decided that Paige was no longer of much use to the team. In 1950, Paige was fired.

Chapter 5

The Pros and Cons of Integration

Many people believed that integration was a good thing, and it was for many African American players and for the future of Major League Baseball. But there were big downsides to integration, too, and not everyone in the black baseball community was happy about it.

The first African Americans to join major league teams were usually the best players on Negro League teams, and as more and more black players were welcomed into the major leagues, the Negro Leagues began to disappear. The quality of play declined, and fans stopped coming to games. As a result, Negro League franchises started to suffer financially, and soon the leagues themselves gradually disappeared.

Paige's career began to decline just as black teams began to disappear. But unlike the time he'd injured his arm, this career shift wasn't upsetting.

The integration of the major leagues brought new opportunities for black baseball players on field, but it also created more opportunities for African Americans off the field.

After his long, storied career, Paige's age was finally catching up with him, but many new opportunities presented themselves in coaching, in publishing, and even in Hollywood. The most exciting opportunity offered to Paige, however, was one of his final moments actually playing, which gave him the chance to go out on top, leaving baseball in a final blaze of glory.

Back to the Majors

When the Kansas City Monarchs heard that Paige was a free agent again, they were eager to sign him. Unfortunately, the Monarchs and other black teams were caught in a downward spiral. Integration of the major leagues had been very bad for the Negro Leagues. As black players broke their contracts to go to the majors, Negro League teams lost their best players. Promising young players began to go straight from high school to minor league farm teams, not stopping to play in the Negro Leagues. But the worst problem was that the fans started to lose interest in the Negro Leagues. All the action was switching to the majors, and Paige hoped that someone would invite him back onto a major league team soon.

In 1951, Bill Veeck bought a new major league team, the St. Louis Browns, and asked Paige to pitch. Paige did not care that the Browns were in last place in their league. He was happy to be in the majors again. He also liked most of his teammates, who respected him and often asked him for advice.

Desperate Times in the Negro Leagues

By the end of the 1940s, most Negro League teams were forced to cut player salaries. Many talented black players who were not able to get into the majors had to play out the rest of their careers outside the United States. The few Negro League teams that did survive into the 1950s and 1960s had to resort to publicity stunts like hiring little people, clowns, and women to play for them. Some teams, like the Indianapolis Clowns, had always focused on entertaining fans as much as playing baseball, and these were the teams that lasted, since their fans came to games for comedy and other entertainment, as well as baseball. After the Negro Leagues folded, the Clowns continued to travel the country on barnstorming tours up through the 1960s. The team continued to play together on and off for exhibition games until it finally disbanded in 1989.

Paige demonstrates his new fastball grip for Cleveland Indians owner Bill Veeck in 1949. Veeck owned the Indians from 1946 to 1950. He also brought Negro League player Larry Doby to the team in 1947.

Roger Hornsby, the Browns' manager, was tough: He treated his players like new recruits in the army. He forced Paige to take part in team practices, run laps, and arrive on time. Paige did not enjoy this strictness at all, but he had to admit that the hard work did him good on the pitching mound. His record was so good that he became the best relief pitcher in baseball that year. He was named to the American League All-Star team in 1952 and 1953, the first African American player to achieve this honor.

Unfortunately, it soon became apparent that Paige's pitching wasn't really strong enough to face major league hitters anymore. His worst year ever came in 1953. When the Browns moved to Baltimore to play with the Orioles, his second major league team took the opportunity to let him go.

Paige still wasn't ready to give up pitching. From 1954 to 1956, he continued to barnstorm and play for the Monarchs. Then, in 1956, he got yet another call from Veeck.

Moving to the Marlins

Over the years, Paige had become less willing to put up with people who treated him badly because of his skin color. Once, a hotel clerk refused to check him into the same hotel with his Browns teammates. Paige went to the airport and took the next plane out of town. His manager called him and begged him to return. Only after Paige got an apology from the hotel did he agree to come back.

The call was about a pitching position with the Miami Marlins. Even though Paige's pitching skills had lessened, he continued to be extremely popular with the fans. Some people said that Veeck was using the old pitcher to get laughs. For Paige's first appearance, Veeck hired a helicopter to drop him off on the baseball field. A rocking chair was set up in the bullpen for Paige to sit in when he wasn't on the mound. The fans really loved these antics, and attendance at the Marlin games was high.

In his first year with the Marlins, Paige proved the critics wrong by pitching pretty well. But after Veeck left the team, Paige couldn't get along with the new owners, especially after they lowered his salary. They added insult to injury by putting him on the inactive list for several months, and by refusing to pay him at all.

Paige desperately wanted to leave the Marlins, but he didn't know how else he would make a living. At fifty-five, he felt he was getting too old to barnstorm, but he had to work. Since he had only played in the majors for a few years, he didn't qualify for the minimum baseball pension of $250 a month, and as usual he didn't have any money in the bank.

The Wonderful Country

Then, in September 1958, an exciting offer came Paige's way. Some Hollywood producers wanted him to play the role of a black cavalry officer in *The Wonderful Country,* a cowboy movie starring Robert Mitchum. Paige and his family were thrilled. The movie was being shot in Mexico, and Lahoma and the kids packed their bags to join Paige on the set.

Paige soon got the hang of acting; he learned to ride a horse and cry for the camera. He told a reporter that he liked the movies because he got to sit down a lot. He also liked the generous pay. If anyone in Hollywood showed any interest in him as an actor, he would be happy to leave baseball behind and embark on a new career as a movie star.

Unfortunately, no more movie offers came Paige's way. For the next six years, he had to continue to pitch for a variety of minor league teams, including the Indianapolis Clowns, the Harlem Globetrotters, and the Portland Beavers. The aging pitcher traveled around in old buses or in his station wagon, staying at a different hotel every night.

Paige shows his pitching technique to a number of boys while on location in Durango, Mexico, for the movie *The Wonderful Country* in 1959.

Paige also found time during this period to write his autobiography, *Maybe I'll Pitch Forever.* Published in 1962, it was filled with both humorous and poignant stories about Paige's life. Paige's version of what had happened in the past often differed from what other people had to say about the same events. The book was very successful and is still in print today.

A Last Hurrah

On September 25, 1965, Paige made his final appearance in a major league game. A publicity-hungry owner, Charles O. Finley, asked the fifty-nine-year-old Paige to pitch one game for his team, the Kansas City Athletics. Many people thought this stunt would be an embarrassment for Paige, and he himself doubted his ability to hold his own against hitters who were forty years younger. But for a paycheck of $5,000, Paige was willing to give it a shot. It turned out to be a triumphant evening for him. In the course of three innings, Paige allowed only one hit, and he struck out seven batters in a row.

After Paige's performance in the Kansas City Athletics game in 1965, owner Charles O. Finley said that he might hire Paige as a pitching coach. Paige needed just 158 more days in the majors to qualify for a pension. But the offer did not come through, and Paige had to keep pitching wherever he could.

In 1968, the Atlanta Braves hired Paige as a pitching coach. The team's owner said that he wanted to make sure Paige qualified for the pension he needed. Paige stayed with the Braves until the required 158 days had passed. He officially retired in 1969, at the age of sixty-three.

Finally, after almost forty years in baseball, Satchel Paige's career had come to an end. What followed his retirement was a long period of stability, honors, and respect—things to which Paige was not accustomed. His post-baseball life included a series of public appearances and celebrity endorsements. During these years, Paige also reached the pinnacle of his career with his induction into the National Baseball Hall of Fame.

Induction into the Hall of Fame

In the 1950s and 1960s, during the civil rights era, African Americans and other minorities began to demand equal rights with white people in American society. As a result, many people turned their attention to segregation in the National Baseball Hall of Fame in Cooperstown, New York. Perhaps the greatest honor that a baseball player can receive is to be voted into the Hall of Fame, but until 1962, when Jackie Robinson was inducted, no black players were enshrined there.

After Paige's retirement in 1969, the Baseball Writers Association of America started a campaign to admit him and other Negro Leaguers into the Hall of Fame. Bill Veeck, Dizzy Dean, Bob Feller, Ted Williams, and others came forward to say how much Paige, in particular, deserved the honor.

Finally, in 1971, the Hall of Fame officials agreed to admit stars of the pre-1974 Negro Leagues. They set up a committee to pick one player from the Negro Leagues every year. Satchel Paige was the committee's first choice.

August 9, 1971, the day on which Paige was inducted into the Hall of Fame, was one of the proudest of his life. In

Paige was the first Negro League player inducted into the Baseball Hall of Fame when he was elected to membership in 1971. Here he stands in front of his Hall of Fame plaque.

his usual style, he gave an entertaining speech at the awards ceremony. He contrasted the praise he was receiving that day with all the bad names that those who were already in the Hall of Fame had called him. He then remarked that baseball had turned him from a second-class citizen into a second-class immortal.

Nearing the End

Paige spent the last ten years of his life living off his celebrity. He settled down with his family in Kansas City, where he spent most of his days out on the town, visiting friends and telling stories in bars. He was hired to promote a minor league team, the Tulsa Oilers. He was inducted into the Missouri Sports Hall of Fame. A TV movie, *Don't Look Back: The Satchel Paige Story,* was made about his life, and he served as a consultant on it. Louis Gossett Jr. played the role of Paige.

In the early 1980s, Paige developed terminal emphysema combined with heart problems. He was confined to a wheelchair, and he had to have an oxygen tank with him at all times.

On June 5, 1982, Paige made his final public appearance. The Kansas City government had cleaned up an abandoned baseball field and named it for him. Paige was deeply touched.

A few days later, on June 8, Paige sent Lahoma, his wife of thirty-five years, to the pharmacy to get some medicine to relieve his chest pains. When she came back, Satchel Paige was dead. He died of a heart attack.

Paige's funeral was held on June 12. There were many celebrities among the 150 mourners. Speeches were made, and articles were written in Paige's honor. Even in death, Paige kept an air of mystery about him. The inscription on his headstone gave his birthdate as "?".

A Legendary Legacy

Satchel Paige was acknowledged as a skilled pitcher, but he was also criticized throughout his career. Some people disliked the way he clowned on the field, lived a wild life, and jumped to a new team every time he was offered a fatter paycheck.

In 1968, Paige was signed to the Atlanta Braves as a pitcher and pitching coach. He did most of his coaching remotely from his home in Kansas City but did play in a few exhibition games.

However, no one could deny that Paige had made enormous contributions to Negro League baseball. Some argue that he even saved it, especially during the Depression. The press made him into a legend, on par with white stars such as Joe DiMaggio. Paige traveled more than anyone else, exposing fans to excellence in black baseball. He helped his teams set attendance records and was often their biggest draw. If he had not been a skilled entertainer, he would not have been able to attract the kind of attention that he did, especially from white fans. And if white fans had not noticed the talented players in black baseball, it probably would have taken a lot longer for African American players to be integrated into the major leagues.

Statistics were not regularly kept in Negro League games, so there is no official record of many of Satchel Paige's stunning achievements. But it has been estimated that he played in about 2,500 games. He claimed to have won 2,000 games, 300 of them shutouts, while pitching for 250 different teams. He is said to have recorded 64 consecutive scoreless innings, a stretch of 21 straight wins, and a 31-4 record in 1933. In Bismarck, North Dakota, he started 29 games in one month (for context, present-day pitchers may start roughly eight games a month at most). In his 179 major league games, Paige did not commit a single error. At the age of forty-two, Paige became the oldest rookie in baseball, winning six of his seven contests and helping the Cleveland Indians to a pennant and a World Series appearance against the Boston Braves. In 1952, at age forty-six, Paige won 12 games with the St. Louis Browns and became the oldest player ever to be selected to the

All-Star team. This impressive record, combined with his unique brand of showmanship, makes it easy to agree with Paige that he may indeed have been the "World's Greatest Pitcher." He was certainly one of the most memorable pitchers the world has ever seen.

Negro Leaguers in the Hall of Fame

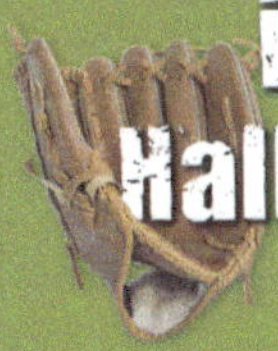

NAME	POSITION	PRIMARY TEAM	DATE INDUCTED
Satchel Paige	Pitcher	Kansas City Monarchs	1971
Josh Gibson	Catcher	Homestead Grays	1972
Buck Leonard	First Baseman	Homestead Grays	1972
Monte Irvin	Left Fielder	Newark Eagles	1973
Cool Papa Bell	Center Fielder	St. Louis Stars	1974
Judy Johnson	Third Baseman	Hilldale Daisies	1975
Oscar Charleston	Center Fielder	Pittsburgh Crawfords	1976
Martín Dihigo	Pitcher	Cuban Stars	1977
Pop Lloyd	Shortstop	New York Lincoln Giants	1977
Rube Foster	Pitcher/Manager	Chicago American Giants	1981
Ray Dandridge	Third Baseman	Newark Eagles	1987
Leon Day	Pitcher	Newark Eagles	1995
Bill Foster	Pitcher	Chicago American Giants	1996
Willie Wells	Shortstop	St. Louis Stars	1997

NAME	POSITION	PRIMARY TEAM	DATE INDUCTED
Bullet Rogan	Pitcher	Kansas City Monarchs	1998
Joe Williams	Pitcher	New York Lincoln Giants	1999
Turkey Stearnes	Center Fielder	Detroit Stars	2000
Hilton Smith	Pitcher	Kansas City Monarchs	2001
Frank Grant	Second Baseman	Cuban Giants	2006
Pete Hill	Center Fielder	Chicago American Giants	2006
José Méndez	Pitcher	Cuban Stars	2006
Louis Santop	Catcher	Hilldale Daisies	2006
Ben Taylor	First Baseman	Indianapolis ABCs	2006
Sol White	Second Baseman/ Executive	Philadelphia Giants	2006
Ray Brown	Pitcher	Homestead Grays	2006
Willard Brown	Outfielder	Kansas City Monarchs	2006
Andy Cooper	Pitcher	Kansas City Monarchs	2006
Biz Mackey	Catcher	Hilldale Giants	2006
Mule Suttles	First Baseman	Newark Eagles	2006
Cristóbal Torriente	Center Fielder	Chicago American Giants	2006
Jud Wilson	Third Baseman	Philadelphia Stars	2006

Timeline

1906

July 7 The day on which Leroy "Satchel" Paige may have been born (and which most people use as his birthdate), in Mobile, Alabama. Neither Paige nor his mother was sure what day or year he was actually born, but a birth certificate for a Leroy Page born on this day is filed in the city of Mobile. A childhood friend claimed that Paige was born in 1900.

1918

Paige is caught shoplifting and is sent to the Industrial School for Negro Children, a reform school, in Mount Meigs, Alabama.

1923

Paige is released from the Industrial School and returns to Mobile.

1924

Paige becomes the star player of the semiprofessional Mobile Tigers.

1926

May 1 Paige makes his professional baseball debut in the Negro Southern League, pitching for the Chattanooga Black Lookouts in a 5–4 victory over the Birmingham Black Barons.

1927

The Chattanooga Black Lookouts trade Paige to the Birmingham Black Barons.

1929

April 29 Paige pitches seventeen strikeouts against the Cuban Stars, beating the then-record in the major leagues of sixteen strikeouts in a game.

1931

Paige joins the Pittsburgh Crawfords, one of the teams in the newly formed Negro National League.

1934

July 4 Paige pitches a no-hitter against the Homestead Grays in Pittsburgh. After the game, he drives to Chicago and shuts out the Chicago American Giants later in the same day, pitching two shutouts in two different cities in one day.

Following one of the best seasons of his career, in which he allowed only 85 hits in 154 innings, Paige earns a spot in the East-West All-Star Game and pitches the East team to victory. Later this year, he breaks his contract with the Crawfords and signs up with the Bismarck Baseball Club, a semiprofessional barnstorming team in North Dakota.

1934

October 26 Paige marries Janet Howard.

1936

Paige returns to the Pittsburgh Crawfords.

1937

Paige plays for a Dominican Republic team, Los Dragones. He soon returns to the Crawfords.

1938

Paige again breaks his contract with the Crawfords to play in Mexico. The Crawfords trade him to the Newark Eagles, but Paige refuses to play for his new team.

1939

Following a long layoff due to an arm injury, Paige begins pitching for the Kansas City Monarchs.

1942

July 21 Paige intentionally walks two hitters in order to load the bases and pitch to Josh Gibson. Before each pitch, he announces what kind of ball he will throw. Despite this warning, Gibson strikes out.

1943

Paige divorces Janet Howard and meets Lahoma Brown.

1948

July 7 Satchel Paige tries out for the Cleveland Indians and earns a spot on the team, becoming the oldest rookie ever to play in the major league. He goes 6-1 in his first major league season, with an ERA of 2.48, earning the honor of Rookie of the Year and helping the Indians reach the World Series.

1951

February 9 Having been released by the Indians in 1950, Paige is signed by the St. Louis Browns.

1952

Following one of Paige's worst seasons, he is released by the Browns, who move to Baltimore and change their name to the Orioles.

1954

Paige returns to the Kansas City Monarchs for two years to barnstorm.

1956

Paige plays for the Negro League Birmingham Black Barons and the minor league Miami Marlins.

1958

September Paige accepts a part in the Hollywood film *The Wonderful Country.*

1962

Paige's autobiography, *Maybe I'll Pitch Forever,* is published.

1965

September 25 Paige makes his final appearance in a major league game, making him baseball's oldest player ever at the age of fifty-nine.

1968

August 11 At sixty-two, Paige is signed by the Atlanta Braves as a pitching coach. This job allows him to qualify for a major league pension.

1969

Paige officially retires from baseball at the age of sixty-three.

1971

August 9 Paige is officially inducted into the Baseball Hall of Fame.

1982

June 5 Paige makes his final public appearance at the dedication of a baseball stadium in Kansas City named after him.

June 8 Paige dies of a heart attack. He is buried on June 12.

Glossary

barnstorming The practice of touring throughout the country to play exhibition games against local teams or other traveling teams, rather than being associated with one city and a home field.

bee ball Also known as pea ball. One of Satchel Paige's fastballs, thrown so fast that it made a buzzing sound.

demeanor A person's outward attitude or behavior.

disband To break up, as an organization.

disciplined To have good control over one's behavior and emotions.

discrimination The unfair treatment of an individual or group of people based on an innate attribute like race or gender.

exhibition game A game played off-season that does not count toward any championship but is designed to generate interest in and enthusiasm for the sport.

farm team A minor league team that is linked to a particular major league team.

fastball The most common type of pitch in baseball. Some pitchers have thrown fastballs over 100 miles per hour.

franchise A professional sports team.

hesitation pitch One of Satchel Paige's trademark pitches, in which he put his foot down before he threw the ball, making it look like he had already thrown it and causing batters to swing too early.

induct To formally accept into a group, usually with a ceremony.

inequity Unfairness; equality happens when situations are equal, but equity happens when situations are fair, which is not always the same thing.

integrated Open to all races, without restriction or discrimination.

Jim Crow Laws intended to keep people of different races separated from each other. These laws established separate institutions for whites and blacks, and the white institutions were of higher quality.

oversight The practice of supervising or organizing something, like a baseball league.

pennant The division or league championship.

racism The belief that one race is superior to others.

racketeer A person who conducts illegal business activities.

rookie A player in their first year on a team.

scout A person, usually a former professional baseball player, who is hired by a professional, major league baseball team to travel to different cities and towns looking for new, young baseball players playing in minor leagues or in semiprofessional ball clubs.

segregation Separation based on race.

semiprofessional Teams in which players have other jobs and only play baseball part-time.

showmanship The skill of being entertaining or extra theatrical.

shutout A game in which one side does not score.

windup The movements of a pitcher before he or she throws the ball.

Further Reading

Books

Democker, Michael. *Barnstorming*. Kennett Square, PA: Purple Toad Publishing, 2016.

Diprimio, Pete. *Legends of the Leagues*. Kennett Square, PA: Purple Toad Publishing, 2016.

Lester, Larry. *Black Baseball in New York City: An Illustrated History, 1885–1959*. Jefferson, NC: McFarland, 2017.

Panchyk, Richard. *Baseball History for Kids*. Chicago, IL: Chicago Review Press, 2016.

Skead, Rob, and Floyd Cooper. *Something to Prove: The Great Satchel Paige vs. Rookie Joe DiMaggio*. Minneapolis, MN: Carolrhoda Books, 2013.

Sturm, James, and Rich Tommaso. *Satchel Paige: Striking Out Jim Crow*. New York, NY: Disney-Hyperion, 2019.

Websites

Major League Baseball's "Negro Leagues Legacy"
mlb.mlb.com/mlb/history/mlb_negro_leagues.jsp
The official website of Major League Baseball offers an archive of Negro League history and images.

National Baseball Hall of Fame
baseballhall.org/hall-of-famers
The Baseball Hall of Fame's official website has historical articles and information about individual Hall of Famers to explore.

Negro Leagues Baseball Museum
www.nlbm.com/s/index.cfm
The Negro Leagues Baseball Museum was founded in 1990 and is located in Kansas City, Missouri.

Satchel Paige: The Official Web Site
www.satchelpaige.com
The official website for Satchel Paige offers a biography, quotations, photos, and statistics from Paige's life and baseball career.

Index

About the Author

Hallie Murray is an editor who lives and works in New York. Originally from New Jersey, she studied English literature at Bowdoin College and Oxford University before beginning her career in publishing at an academic press. Outside of work, she enjoys ultimate Frisbee and long-distance running. She also loves cooking, music, and the *New York Times* crossword.